Write On

Activity Book 3
9-11 years

Introduction

Write On 3 contains activities especially designed for children between nine and eleven years old. Many children at this stage will be increasingly fluent writers, aware of different styles of writing and confident in choosing and using forms of writing to suit their needs. Some children will have begun to develop a strong personal style which incorporates an ever-growing vocabulary. Activities in this booklet aim to revise, consolidate and extend children's ability to craft language to suit their purpose and audience through the following areas:

- creating contexts for purposeful writing
- experiencing a range of literary styles
- narrative forms of writing
- information writing
- use of book language
- development of personal style or voice as an author
- writing conventions
- opportunities to plan and redraft
- writing response partners
- shared reading and writing as a model
- drawing on a range of sources to inform writing
- developing expression of ideas
- developing an awareness of the effect of grammar, punctuation and spelling on the meaning and communication of writing.

The Literacy Hour's focus on text, sentence and word level work has been reflected in the content and structure of activities in this booklet.

Detailed teacher's notes commence with ideas for directed class work, independent and collaborative group work.

Shared texts suitable for class work and individual reference are used throughout to introduce children to a range of literary styles. These texts can also be used as a basis to explore how different authors develop for example character and plot, and their choice of word and style to shape the story or poem.

Shared writing is suggested throughout as an opportunity for the teacher to model the writing process and to focus explicitly on particular elements they wish to teach. Through it children can learn about the composition and processes of writing as dictated by purpose and audience, as well as the conventions of print and transcription.

Plenary sessions are integral to each activity. They encourage the children to share their work, build confidence and develop a sense of audience in a mutually respectful environment. Through comment and discussion children will develop a deeper understanding of the writing process and learn how to support one another.

All activities are marked to indicate levels of difficulty and have clearly defined learning intentions for teacher and parent reference.

Differentiation is by outcome and space is provided for teachers' comments on this.

Write On 3 contains 28 activity sheets organised into four sections: Book focus (a focus on the conventions, structure and forms of narrative writing), Poetry, Writing for a range of purposes, and Story writing.

Contents

Teachers' notes

Section 1: Book focus 2
Section 2: Poetry 4
Section 3: Writing for a range of purposes 5
Section 4: Story writing 6

Activity sheets

Section 1: Book focus
1 Beginnings 8
2 Endings 9
3 Writing dialogue 10
4 A problem 11
5 Comparing characters 12
6 Character study 13
7 Describing settings 14
8 The new classmate 15

Section 2: Poetry
1 Riddles 16
2 Haiku 17
3 List poems 18
4 Shape poems 19
5 Concerns 20
6 Knocking at the door 21

Section 3: Writing for a range of purposes
1 Applying for a job 22
2 Recipe 23
3 Cities 24
4 Weather 25
5 Volcanoes 26
6 Hot-air balloons 27
7 Researching information 28

Section 4: Story writing
1 Story pots 29
2 Newspaper report 30
3 Story style 31
4 Science fiction 32
5 Planning sheet 33
6 Drafting your work 34
7 Writing response partner 35

Individual achievement award 36
Other resources Inside back cover

Section 1: Book focus

Extracts from books by familiar children's authors are used to help children focus on the structures and conventions of story. Children are encouraged to explore the integral elements of story, character development and use of dialogue.

key: Extension activity — Difficulty level 1 2 — Level of difficulty

Beginnings
page 8

Learning intentions and resources
- Children write an opening paragraph of their own, using the three extracts given on the sheet as models.
- Focus: awareness of author style, writing opening paragraphs, imaginative writing.
- Resources: thesauri.

Class work
- Read the extracts and discuss what makes them good beginnings.
- Ask children which book they would choose to read. Ask the children to identify what appeals to them and why.
- Model an opening paragraph as shared writing.

Grouping, activity and extension
- Children work alone.
- Children think carefully about the style they will choose.
- Children write their opening paragraph.
- Children write another in a different style.

Plenary
- Read the range of openings.
- Identify successful parts and effective words or phrases.

Role of the teacher
- Encourage children to be self-critical and redraft where necessary.
- Encourage children to read their passages aloud to their response partner.

Difficulty level 1 2 3

Endings
page 9

Learning intentions and resources
- Children are asked to read two extracts outlining different dilemmas and write a suitable ending for one of them.
- Focus: imaginative writing, creating a suitable ending, awareness of author style.
- Resources: range of fiction books.

Class work
- Read the extracts.
- Ask children to explore possible endings for the first extract verbally.
- Develop endings through shared writing.

Grouping, activity and extension
- Children work alone.
- Children reread a selection of endings in fiction books they have read before.
- Children analyse these endings. They should think about how descriptions are made and how emotions are evoked and explore the detail.
- Children finish the second ending. They should model their ending on what they have found out from the selected fiction.

Plenary
- Share some of the endings.
- Discuss the effectiveness and consider the variety of endings offered.
- Discuss the notion of ownership in writing and the control an author has over a story.

Role of the teacher
- Emphasise the need for the reader to feel satisfied with the ending. Children need to ensure that they carry the reader with them and that the reader empathises with the author.

Difficulty level 3

Writing dialogue
page 10

Learning intentions and resources
- Using an extract as a stimulus, children are asked to write a dialogue between a teacher and a pupil.
- Focus: writing dialogue.

Class work
- Discuss the setting and characters.
- Discuss the characters' vocabulary and 'tone of voice'.
- Explore some inventive excuses that Michael might use and the responses Mr Jackson would give.
- Revise the writing conventions for dialogue.

Grouping, activity and extension
- Children work alone.
- Children consider how they think the dialogue would develop.
- Children craft a plan of their ideas.
- Children write out the full dialogue, taking into consideration the conventions of writing.
- (Extension) Children write a dialogue of the conversation Mr Jackson might have about Michael's behaviour with another teacher in the staffroom.

Plenary
- Invite children to read aloud their dialogues.
- The dialogues could be used as scripts for performance.
- Invite responses from the class.

Role of the teacher
- Encourage children to be original and imaginative in their writing.
- Help children to consider writing conventions and layout.

Difficulty level 1 2 3

A problem
page 11

Learning intentions and resources
- Children consider the problems of the character depicted in the extract and draft a letter to a magazine seeking advice. This sheet will also be used with the next sheet, 'Comparing characters'.
- Focus: character study, assuming the 'voice' of the character, imaginative writing.
- Resources: suitable examples from problem pages of magazines.

Class work
- Read the passage aloud.
- Ask the children to identify the character traits described in the passage.
- Discuss how the character's 'inner' self has affected her 'outer' self.
- Discuss the roles of agony aunts.

Grouping, activity and extension
- Children work in pairs.
- Children consider the character of Julia and the content of a letter to an agony aunt.
- (Extension) Children write the agony aunt's reply to Julia, trying to give advice that will solve her problems.

Plenary
- Share the letters.
- Discuss emotional responses evoked while listening to the letters.

Role of the teacher
- Encourage children to put themselves in Julia's place before composing the letter.

Difficulty level 2 3

Comparing characters
page 12

Learning intentions and resources
- This activity sheet is designed to be used with the extract from the previous activity sheet. Children compare the two characters in the extracts. This work will be used in the next sheet, 'Character study'.
- Focus: character study and effect on plot.
- Resources: extract from previous activity sheet.

Class work
- Read the extract from *The Daydreamer*.
- Consider the character of Peter.
- Reread the extract from *The Runaways*.
- Compare the two characters. How would they interact with children, teachers and other adults?

Grouping, activity and extension
- Children work alone or in pairs.
- Children consider or discuss the two characters.
- Children consider how the characters would react to situations and other people.
- Children make a list to show how the characters' days are different.

Plenary
- Read some accounts aloud.
- How well were the characters contrasted?

Role of the teacher
- Try to get children to 'step into the shoes' of each character.

Difficulty level 2 3

Character study
page 13

Learning intentions and resources
- Children are asked to reflect on the depictions of Julia and Peter from previous sheets. They are then asked to consider someone from their class as a focus for writing a character study.
- Focus: character study, seeing people from another perspective, descriptive language.

Class work
- Revise work on the characters of Julia and Peter.
- Ask children to consider someone in their class who is different from themselves for the character study.
- Explain that they must not name the child.
- They must consider the character's point of view, thoughts and feelings.

Grouping, activity and extension
- Children work alone.
- Children choose someone different from themselves.
- Children write a character study of the chosen child.
- Children should not write a character study that would upset others.
- Children consider the person carefully and make notes before writing.
- Children choose an imaginary name for their character.

Plenary
- Carefully select accounts to read out.

Role of the teacher
- Remind children of the effective use of, for example, similes to paint a vivid picture.
- Ensure that children do not write a character study that would upset others.

Difficulty level 1 2 3

Describing settings
page 14

Learning intentions and resources
- Children are asked to read the extract describing a kitchen. Using this as a stimulus, they must write a description of a room they know well.
- Focus: scene-setting, descriptive language, awareness of audience.

Class work
- Read the extract aloud.
- Discuss the effectiveness of painting a picture in the reader's mind.
- Draw attention to the selection of detailed information.
- Encourage children to focus on an area of the classroom and give verbal descriptions to write as a shared writing activity.

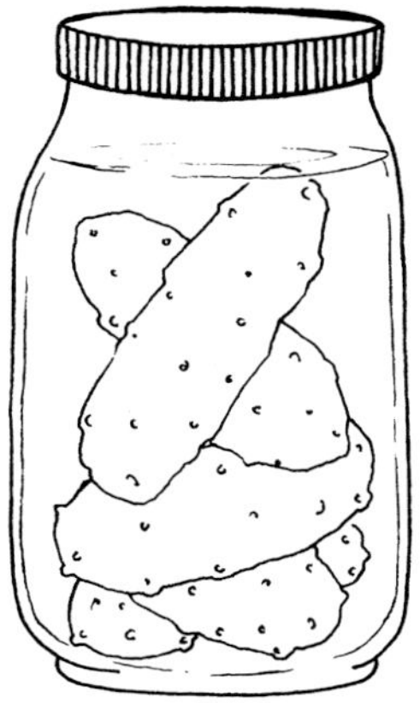

Grouping, activity and extension
- Children work alone.
- Children describe a room that they know well.
- Children consider their audience and write an account that will enable the reader to picture the room in his or her mind.
- Children describe other areas such as a garden, the street where they live or the school playground.

Plenary
- Ask children to read their work aloud.
- How did the other children respond? Were they able to picture the room? What parts did they like best? Which parts worked well?

Role of the teacher
- Give advice on suitable vocabulary.
- Remind children to include some detail.
- Help children redraft sections to make them more interesting and personal. For example, changing 'There's a cupboard with toys in it' to 'The cupboard under the window opens out displaying my most precious possessions: toys that will carry me to far-off places and on amazing adventures'.

Difficulty level 1 2 3

The new classmate
page 15

Learning intentions and resources
- Children are asked to imagine that a new girl or boy has arrived at the school and has been asked to sit next to them. They need to recount what they imagine would happen on each day of that first week.
- Focus: imaginative writing, diary writing, personal accounts, sequencing events, developing character.

Class work
- Discuss the purposes of a diary to recall events, emotions.
- Discuss how the children must imagine the new person and how s/he interacts with their own lives. What sort of character they will invent: someone shy or confident, happy or miserable, someone interesting, a bully, etc?
- Demonstrate how to make the diary by cutting out and folding into zigzag, with Monday and Tuesday on the front and the other days on the back.
- Cut off strip to make a fastener for the diary.

Grouping, activity and extension
- Children work alone.
- Children fold main body of paper into zigzag diary and write in extra days.
- Children imagine the new classmate. What will be their first impressions? How might their thoughts change over the week?
- Children write the diary from their own point of view, imagining their observations of the new classmate.
- Children cut strip off. When the diary is finished, they will use this strip to it secure by weaving through slits.
- Children write the diary from the point of view of the new classmate.

Plenary
- Ask children to read out their diary entries.
- How well did they develop events and characters?

Role of the teacher
- Encourage children to develop the new classmate's character over the week.
- Encourage children to include events that will show the development of their own responses to the new classmate.

Difficulty level 1 2 3

Section 2: Poetry

A diverse collection of poetry broadens children's experience of this genre. They are challenged to extend and refine their knowledge and choice of vocabulary, in order to craft poems of their own.

Riddles
page 16

Learning intentions and resources
- Children read riddle poems and guess the subjects. They write a riddle of their own, shaping it as a poem.
- Focus: careful use of vocabulary, descriptive writing, poetry writing.
- Resources: dictionaries, thesauri, riddle books.

Class work
- Share and enjoy the riddles.
- Talk about who the riddle will be written for.
- Discuss the structure of riddles and how the vocabulary is designed to give hints (but nothing more than hints).
- Suggest use of similes, kennings, etc.

Grouping, activity and extension
- Children work alone or in pairs.
- Children decide on their subject and jot ideas down.
- Children select and shape ideas into a riddle poem.

Plenary
- Share and enjoy a selection of the finished riddles.
- Discuss the effectiveness of the vocabulary used.

Role of the teacher
- Remind children that the riddle is supposed to be a puzzle for the reader to guess: the subject should not be obvious too early on.

Difficulty level 1 2 3

Haiku
page 17

Learning intentions and resources
- Children use examples of haiku poetry as a model for writing their own haiku.
- Focus: succinct language, visual imagery, syllable awareness, poetry writing.
- Resources: a collection of haiku poems.

Class work
- Read the examples and discuss the visual imagery that is evoked.
- Explain the structure of haiku and revise work on syllables.
- Use shared writing to model examples.
- Try to keep to the syllabic structure.

Grouping, activity and extension
- Children work alone or in pairs.
- Children choose a subject suitable for a haiku.
- Children consider the use of language and write the haiku.

Plenary
- Read some of children's haiku.
- Discuss the range of subjects and how they were approached.
- Discuss whether the structure of the haiku is helpful or limiting.

Role of the teacher
- Stress the importance of careful selection of individual words.
- Remind children that a haiku paints a picture.
- Encourage use of syllabic structure but allow for slight variations.

Difficulty level 1 2 3

List poems
page 18

Learning intentions and resources
- Children compose a list poem of their own, using the examples given on the sheet as models.
- Focus: extending experience of range of poetry writing, visual imagery, brevity of language.
- Resources: other list-like poetry.

Class work
- Read the examples.
- Discuss the structure of these poems.
- Compose a class poem as shared writing to demonstrate the activity.
- Discuss the importance of choice of words and of keeping the 'items' brief.
- Encourage children to conclude with a satisfactory last line.

Grouping, activity and extension
- Children work alone or in pairs.
- Children select a suitable subject and title.
- Children compile the list poem.
- Children compile an anthology of list poems. For example, an anthology called *School Poems* could include 'Assembly', 'Maths', 'Playtime', etc.

Plenary
- Share and enjoy the poems created.
- Ask children to identify which parts of the poems were most successful.

Role of the teacher
- Remind children to consider detail.

Difficulty level 1 2 3

Shape poems
page 19

Learning intentions and resources
- Children compose a poem formed into the shape of its subject, using the shape poems on the sheet as models.
- Focus: styles of poetry, presentation.

Class work
- Read the examples on the sheet.
- Discuss the structure and shape of the poems. The way in which the words work down through the shape can be skewed, as in the kite poem.
- Compose a shape poem through shared writing.

Grouping, activity and extension
- Children work alone or in pairs.
- Children select the subject and title.
- Children brainstorm words or phases linked to title. They should consider the shape and arrange their thoughts to work within the shape.

Plenary
- Discuss the success of the activity and share any difficulties.
- Compile into a class book or display.

Role of the teacher
- Ensure children brainstorm words or phases linked to title before attempting the shape.

Snake
glides
through
grass,
over
pebbles,
forked
tongue
working,
never
speaking
but its
body
whispers,
listen

Difficulty level 1 2 3

Concerns
page 20

Learning intentions and resources
- Children read poems that raise environmental issues. They are then asked to compose a poem dealing with similar issues.
- Focus: poetry used to raise awareness and provoke a response.

Class work
- Read the poems on the sheet.
- Discuss the environmental issues raised.
- Discuss emotional responses to the poems.
- Discuss styles and structures of the poems and what makes them so successful. How does the last line of each poem create the final punch?

Grouping, activity and extension
- Children work alone or in pairs.
- Children consider an environmental concern. This could be global or local.
- Children jot their thoughts down on paper.
- Children shape their thoughts into a poem.

Plenary
- Share the children's poems.
- Discuss their effectiveness.
- Compile an anthology.

Role of the teacher
- Help children to focus on a specific issue such as pollution, deforestation, declining animal population, disappearance of habitats, etc.

Difficulty level 1 2 3

Section 3: Writing for a range of purposes

This section offers opportunities to write for a wide range of purposes. Challenging tasks demand that children search for the appropriate language and style to suit their purpose and audience.

Knocking at the door page 21

Learning intentions and resources

- The children read two poems and write a poem on a similar subject.
- Focus: evoking atmosphere, writing a story-type poem, imaginative writing.

Class work

- Read the poems on the sheet.
- Discuss each poem in depth. When would they have been written? Where are they set? etc.
- **'The Listeners'** Who are the listeners? Why is the house deserted? Who had lived there? Who is the traveller and why has he come late at night? What promise could he have made?
- **'Someone'** Was anyone really there? Who could have knocked on the door?
- Discuss the atmosphere evoked in both poems.
- Discuss the structure, rhythm and style of each poem.

Grouping, activity and extension

- Children work alone.
- Children read the poems.
- Children consider the 'story'. Where and when was it set?
- Children think about being alone at night.
- Children compose a night-time poem that tells an unfinished story, making it as eerie as possible.

Plenary

- Read the children's poems.
- Discuss which felt most eerie and how this atmosphere was achieved.

Role of the teacher

- Encourage children to think about developing an eerie atmosphere.

Difficulty level 1 2 3

Applying for a job page 22

Learning intentions and resources

- Children are asked to write a formal letter in response to one of the job advertisements on the activity sheet.
- Focus: letter writing, formal layout and style, suitable language, writing for a specific purpose.
- Resources: dictionaries and thesauri.

Class work

- Discuss the formal language used in business letters. Discuss the 'tone' of the letter.
- Discuss the points on the sheet.
- Demonstrate the activity to show layout of formal letters and the style and language used.

Grouping, activity and extension

- Children work alone or in pairs.
- Children read the advertisements and choose one to apply for.
- Children write a letter, bearing in mind the points on the activity sheet.
- Children role-play an interview.

Plenary

- Read and discuss the letters, highlighting interesting and useful phrases.
- Discuss the difficulty of writing in formal language.

Role of the teacher

- Monitor the task.
- Help children to write in a formal style.

Difficulty level 1 2 3

Recipe page 23

Learning intentions and resources

- Children are asked to convert information from a storyboard format into a complete recipe.
- Focus: style of writing, writing for a specific purpose.
- Resources: recipe books.

Class work

- Discuss the specific writing style for a recipe: listing the ingredients and writing the method step by step.
- Discuss the need for accuracy of weights, ingredients, cooking time, etc.
- Outline the task.

Grouping, activity and extension

- Children work alone.
- Children write out the recipe for making these scones.
- Children decorate their recipe if they wish.
- Children write out their favourite recipe from home.

Plenary

- How clear was the layout?
- How easy was it to follow the instructions?

Role of the teacher

- Ensure that children check ingredients and stages.

Difficulty level 1 2 3

Cities page 24

Learning intentions and resources

- Children are asked to look up places in an atlas, search for information and transfer this information to a grid. They are then asked to provide written answers and pose questions of their own.
- Focus: developing writing for research purposes, answering in full sentences, posing written questions.
- Resources: atlases.

Class work

- Advise on how to use an atlas.
- Demonstrate how to search for places and find the relevant information.
- Discuss how to plot information on a grid.
- Discuss how to answer questions as full sentences and ask children to pose questions.

Grouping, activity and extension

- Children work in pairs.
- Children search for each city and transfer the necessary information on to the grid.
- Children answer the questions.
- Children pose questions for their partner to answer.
- Children make a similar grid and questions on, for example, wild cats.

Plenary

- How successful were children at transferring the information on to a grid?
- Did they answer the questions in complete sentences?
- What sort of questions did they pose?

Role of the teacher

- Advise on use of index and grid reference.
- Support children with transferring the information.

Difficulty level 1 2 3

Weather page 25

Learning intentions and resources

- Children look at a weather map. Using the information on the map, they write a forecast for each area.
- Focus: interpreting pictorial information in a written form, use of appropriate vocabulary, writing succinctly.
- Resources: weather maps from newspapers.

Class work

- Discuss the style of language used by weather forecasters.
- Brainstorm as many 'weather' words as possible (they could be researched from newspapers).
- Discuss the symbols used on weather maps.
- Discuss the areas on the map and example given.

Grouping, activity and extension

- Children work alone.
- Children take each region one at a time and look on the map to see what symbols there are for this region.
- Children write a forecast based on the symbols. They should try to write it so that areas with the same weather don't all read exactly the same.
- Children make up a map of their own.

Plenary

- Discuss the variety and range of weather statements.
- How many different ways are there of saying the same thing?

Role of the teacher

- Help children to distinguish regions on the map.

Difficulty level 1 2 3

Section 4: Story writing

This section encourages children to extend and manipulate their knowledge of the elements of story to maximise their impact on the reader. They do this through experience of genre, defining settings, interactive characters, use of detail and coherent story lines, etc.

Volcanoes
page 26

Learning intentions and resources
- Children are asked to extract information from a diagram of an active volcano and present it as a written account.
- Focus: writing for information, changing pictorial information to a written account, using specialised vocabulary.

Class work
- Discuss the processes involved when a volcano becomes active.
- Explain the glossary and how children can use it to assist them in their task.

Grouping, activity and extension
- Children work alone or pairs.
- Children write an account of volcanic action using the information on the sheet.
- Children research volcanic action on, for example, the island of Monserrat. They present their information to the class.

Plenary
- Invite children to read their accounts.
- Discuss any difficulties and how they were overcome.

Role of the teacher
- Give further explanation to those children who require it.
- Encourage and support individual children.

Difficulty level 3

Hot-air balloons
page 27

Learning intentions and resources
- Children read an account and have to rewrite it as if they were a television reporter.
- Focus: writing for another purpose, imaginative writing, extending range of writing, considering audience.

Class work
- Discuss the styles of television news reporting. How do reporters introduce and finish their report? How do they conduct brief interviews? How do they attract and keep the attention of the audience? etc.
- Discuss the account of the first manned balloon flight. Consider what a sensational event it would have been.

Grouping, activity and extension
- Children work in pairs.
- Children read the account.
- Children discuss the event.
- Children consider how to write it up as news report for television in a way that keeps the viewers watching.
- With others, children role-play the event. They could write down their role play as a script for a play.

Plenary
- Ask children to give their news reports as if the event were unfolding behind them.

Role of the teacher
- Encourage children to imagine that they are talking directly into the microphone and to the camera.
- Encourage children to write their report 'as it happens'.

Difficulty level 2 3

Researching information
page 28

Learning intentions and resources
- This activity sheet is a framework to help children structure their study skills and information writing. It could be linked with the previous sheet on hot-air balloons. The sheet is designed to be used at any stage in children's learning. It could be used to aid assessment.
- Focus: to demonstrate what children know, what they need to find out and where to find it.

Class work
- Discuss how this activity sheet can help children plan a topic.
- Demonstrate how to use the sheet.

Grouping, activity and extension
- Children write down all the things they know about their chosen topic.
- Children brainstorm ideas about what they would like to find out about. These can be written as questions.
- Children research the topic and write down what they found out.
- Children note where they found the information.

Plenary
- Discuss how well children were able to find the information they wanted and how effectively they recorded their findings.
- Can they select key words to aid research?

Role of the teacher
- Encourage children to use the sheet regularly as a basis for research. They can change the headings to suit their needs.

Difficulty level 1 2 3

Story pots
page 29

Learning intentions and resources
- Children select ingredients from the pots on the sheet to weave into a story of their own.
- Focus: creative writing, development of character, setting and plot, imaginative use of language.

Class work
- Talk through the elements of good story writing.
- Stress the need for detail to bring the story to life.
- Stress the importance of imaginative language.
- Discuss the list on the activity sheet and the need for careful planning.
- Model a plan as shared writing, using some ingredients from the story pots.

Grouping, activity and extension
- Children work alone.
- Children select ingredients carefully to weave into the story.
- Children plan the story before writing it out in full.
- After careful redrafting and editing, children add illustrations to make their story into a book for others to read.

Plenary
- Read aloud a selection of stories or excerpts that children are pleased with.
- Encourage others to comment on the parts they enjoyed.

Role of the teacher
- Encourage children to be self-critical and redraft their work.

Difficulty level 1 2 3

Newspaper report
page 30

Learning intentions and resources
- Children are asked to write a newspaper report. They are given a speech as a clue to the setting and characters they need to include.
- Focus: selecting appropriate characters, writing a newspaper report, attention to tense and style.

Class work
- Using the report on the activity sheet as a model, discuss the style, characters involved, setting and use of quotes.

Grouping, activity and extension
- Children work alone.
- Children read the speech.
- Children consider where they think the speech takes place, who they think would be speaking, who would have organised the event and who would be in the crowd watching.
- Children write up their report for a newspaper. They should consider headlines, columns, pictures, etc.
- Children complete the full page of the newspaper, thinking about what other articles or features would be on the page.

Plenary
- Invite children to read out their reports.
- How do their reports differ? How was the story reported?

Role of the teacher
- Encourage children to consider a variety of people who might be there.

Difficulty level 1 2 3

Story style
page 31

Learning intentions and resources
- A story is given on the sheet. It is in sections. Only the first lines of each section are given. Children are asked to read the start of each section of the story and identify the genre. They then develop the story to its conclusion.
- Focus: identifying genre of story and its style and tense, linking sections, writing suitable endings.

Class work
- Read each section of the story. Discuss how they could develop. Explain that each section must link to the next.
- Discuss the tense used.

Grouping, activity and extension
- Children work alone.
- Children identify what sort of story it is.
- Children continue each section and link it to the opening of the next. (Use separate sheets of paper for longer stories.)
- Children think of a suitable ending for the story.

Plenary
- How well did children identify the genre used?
- Read the stories and discuss the range and variety.
- How well did the children keep to the style and tense?
- Read out especially effective sections.

Role of the teacher
- Encourage children to think about planning how they will continue from the first lines given and what characters they might introduce.
- Encourage children to continue the style and tense throughout.

Difficulty level 1 2 3

Science fiction
page 32

Learning intentions and resources
- Children are given a framework for writing a science fiction story that they use to write their own story.
- Focus: genre and style of writing, continuing and linking sections, writing suitable endings.

Class work
- Discuss the science fiction genre.
- Invite children for suggestions as to what might happen in each section.

Grouping, activity and extension
- Children work alone.
- Children read the introduction to each section.
- Children continue each section, making links between sections.
- Children write a suitable ending for the story.

Children write starting points in another genre for a partner to continue.

Plenary
- Invite children to read their stories.
- Discuss the range of outcomes.
- Discuss effective sections and smooth links.

Role of the teacher
- Encourage children to think about planning how they will continue and what characters they might introduce.
- Encourage children to keep a flow through their writing.

Difficulty level 1 2 3

Planning sheet
page 33

Learning intentions and resources
- This sheet is designed to help children plan work and incorporate detail for the first draft of their work. It can be used with the next two sheets, 'Drafting your work' and 'Writing response partner'.
- Focus: improving written work, selecting and attending to specific elements of writing.

Class work
- Discuss how the sheet can help children write.
- Discuss the planning section.
- Model a plan, working through the suggestions on the activity sheet.
- Discuss drafting of work and how plans need revising.

Grouping, activity and extension
- Children work alone.
- Children use the sheet to help plan out their work.
- Children check they have paid attention to all the points.
- Children incorporate any ideas into their first draft and revise plan if necessary.

Plenary
- Discuss how well the children paid attention to the sheet.
- Discuss what they found most useful.
- Did it help remind them of aspects they hadn't thought of?

Role of the teacher
- Encourage children to use the sheet regularly.

Difficulty level 1 2 3

Drafting your work
page 34

Learning intentions and resources
- This sheet is designed to help children attend to the detail of the first draft of their work. This draft is then passed on to a response partner (see next sheet, 'Writing response partner') for comments before final draft.
- Focus: improving written work, proofreading.

Class work
- Discuss how the sheet can help children write.
- Discuss drafting of work.
- Discuss response partners and their role.
- Discuss final draft.

Grouping, activity and extension
- Children work in pairs.
- Children carefully go through the first draft, checking they have gone through all the points.
- Children hand their work to their response partner and listen to what the partner has to say.
- Children incorporate any good ideas into their draft.
- Children write out a final draft.

Plenary
- Discuss how well the children paid attention to the sheet.
- Discuss what they found most useful.
- Did it help remind them of aspects they hadn't thought of?

Role of the teacher
- Encourage children to use the sheet regularly.

Difficulty level 1 2 3

Writing response partner
page 35

Learning intentions and resources
- Children are asked to become a writing response partner. They can use the sheet to help them focus on someone else's writing.
- Focus; proofreading, providing positive support to others, paying attention to detail of writing.

Class work
- Discuss the notion of response partners and how it can inform their own as well as their partner's work.
- Discuss the role of a response partner: to be encouraging and supportive and to offer positive criticism.
- Discuss how they can use positive language when offering suggestions or pointing out spelling errors.

Grouping, activity and extension
- Children work in pairs.
- Children read their partner's work carefully.
- Children go through the points on the activity sheet and address each one in turn.
- Children give encouragement and support to their partner. They should think positively!

Plenary
- Discuss how the sheets help children to focus on their partner's work.

Role of the teacher
- Ensure children do not respond negatively or ridicule their partner's work.
- Encourage children to use the sheets regularly.

Difficulty level 1 2 3

Name Date

Read the beginnings from these three stories.

Challenge in the Dark
by Robert Leeson

Monday morning. Dad came yawning up the stairs as I came yawning down. He was coming off night shift ready for a good day's sleep. I was starting my first week at the big school. I'd have gladly changed places, but they don't take you on British Rail at eleven.

The Ghost of Thomas Kempe
by Penelope Lively

James Harrison and his mother turned out of Ledsham's main street into a lane tht ran between the terraced cottages. The lane ended abruptly at a gate and became a footpath which disappeared in a landscape of fields and trees, ridged with the dark lines of hedges. Their own cottage stood at the end: the last house in Ledsham. It was called East End Cottage and they had been living there for two weeks.

Two Weeks with the Queen
by Morris Gleitzman

The Queen looked out across the Mudford's living-room and wished everyone a happy Christmas.

Colin scowled.

Easy for you, he thought. Bet you got what you wanted. Bet if you wanted a microscope you got a microscope. Bet your tree was covered in microscopes. Bet nobody gave you daggy school shoes for Christmas.

This extract takes you immediately into the dilemma of the story: starting secondary school.

This extract tells you what the setting of the story is.

This extract raises the curiosity of the reader.

Choose a location or setting for a story. You could choose a deserted beach, a haunted house or an empty school. Plan your story and write an opening paragraph. How will you introduce the characters, set the mood and grab the reader's attention?

Learning intentions
To focus on the opening paragraph of a story.
To interpret style of other authors and what they are trying to achieve.
To write an opening paragraph and consider how to set the scene.

Outcomes

Difficulty level
1 2 3

Write On 3

Read these passages carefully. They all describe dilemmas (problems).

Noah's Brother
by Dick King-Smith

In this extract from *Noah's Brother*, the ark is ready to go and Noah is giving orders to his sons.

'Pull up the gangway!' he shouted, and Shem, Ham and Jaspheth pulled it up.

'Hey!' cried Noah's brother as the storm roared; 'Hey! Hang on a minute! What about me?'

But nobody seemed to hear.

The Fib
by George Layton

I didn't dare say another word. What was I going to do about my jelly? I had to bring one. I'd promised. There was only one thing for it. I'd have to make one myself. So I decided to wait until my mum went to bed, and then I'd go downstairs and make one. I don't know how to keep awake. I'm sure I nodded off once or twice, but after a while I heard my mum switch her light off and when I'd given her time to get to sleep, I crept downstairs.

Select one of these dilemmas and write an ending which will resolve it so that it comes to a satisfactory conclusion.

Learning intentions
To write imaginatively.
To draw events to a close and develop a satisfactory conclusion.
To identify dilemmas and consider the emotions of characters.

Outcomes

Difficulty level 3

Writing dialogue

Name Date

Challenge in the Dark
by Robert Leeson

While Mr Jackson was dismissing us, I got my stuff together under my desk, looking straight at him as though I was listening very hard to what he was saying about something we needed for the next day. But who cared about tomorrow? Today was enough for me. I pressed down with my feet and hands like a runner waiting for the starting gun and the second Mr. Jackson stopped talking I was away across the room like a rocket. Taylor stuck his foot out, but I gave his ankle a sideways tap (as shown on 'Match of the Day') and nipped out sharpish. I could hear Mr. Jackson shouting 'Come BACK, Michael,' but I kept going.

Read the passage carefully. Michael is being bullied by Taylor. He has been threatened with a beating after school, so he dashes out early. The next morning he will have to explain his actions.
Make a plan on the back of this sheet to outline the scene you imagine may take place the next day. Write the dialogue you imagine will take place between Mr Jackson and Michael.

Learning intentions
To consider and write dialogue between two characters.
To use appropriate punctuation for dialogue.
To consider the effects of plot and character on writing dialogue.
To write dialogue suited to the characters.

Outcomes

Difficulty level 1 2 3

Name Date

Read this passage carefully.

The Runaways
by Ruth Thomas

Julia was an only child. When she first came to school she was five years old and had never played with other children, so she had no idea how to behave with them.

She grabbed all the crayons for herself, pinched the other children and whined complaints all day. So gradually the others turned against her, and no-one wanted to play with her. Nowadays Julia no longer pinched people or took their pencils. Indeed, she was rather afraid of them. There were so many of them, and only one of her. But somehow she had never been able to live down those early mistakes. And now, with her face set permanently in an expression of slightly anxious unhappiness and her shoulders hunched up into a despondent stoop, Julia was a fairly unattractive sight as well. She thought she was ugly, which she wasn't. Not pretty of course, but not exactly ugly. Actually she had rather nice teeth, but since she hardly ever opened her mouth to smile very few people had noticed. Julia herself had no idea how much difference a real smile would have made.

Julia had many problems, the most important being that she had no friends.
Imagine you are Julia. Write to a magazine for advice. Try to outline the problems you have.

Learning intentions
To 'step into the shoes' of a character and write from the character's point of view.
To consider the emotional state of the character.
To compose a letter using imaginary thoughts in keeping with the character.
To write using the 'voice' of the character.

Outcomes

Difficulty level 2 3

Comparing characters

Name Date

The Daydreamer
by Ian McEwan

'Peter, Peter! What are you thinking about?' they would call to him. And Peter would sit up with a start. 'Oh, nothing. Nothing at all.' Grown-ups knew that something was going on inside his head, but they couldn't hear it or see it or feel it. They couldn't tell Peter to stop it, because they did not know what it was he was doing in there. He could have been setting his school on fire or feeding his sister to an alligator and escaping in a hot-air balloon, but all they saw was a boy staring at the blue sky without blinking, a boy who did not hear you when you called his name.

As for being on his own, grown-ups didn't like that much either. They don't even like other grown-ups being on their own. When you join in, people can see what you're up to. You're up to what they're up to. You have to join in, or you'll spoil it for everyone else. Peter had different ideas. Joining in was all very fine in its place. But far too much of it went on. In fact, he thought, if people spent less time joining in and making others join in, and spent a little time each day alone remembering who they were or who they might be, then the world would be a happier place and wars might never happen.

At school he often left his body sitting at its desk while his mind went off on its journey.

Peter from *The Daydreamer* and Julia from *The Runaways* both spent time on their own but for very different reasons. Compare what you think their responses might be to doing all the different things that may happen during a school day: PE, assembly, playtime, maths, group work, lunch-time and silent reading.

Write down your ideas on the back of this sheet in a table like this:

Peter's day	Julia's day

Learning intentions
To explore character development.
To compare and contrast characters.
To consider how character affects plot.
To write imaginatively.

Outcomes

Difficulty level 2 3

Write On 3

Name Date

Peter in *The Daydreamer* and Julia in *The Runaways* had very different characters. Every class has many children, all of them different, with different feelings and emotions, who react differently to the other children and adults around.

Look around your classroom. Choose someone you think has a very different character to your own.

- Is he or she more confident than you or is he or she quiet and shy?
- What do you think he or she is thinking and feeling?
- Are there ways in which he or she is similar to yourself?
- Think of him or her in the playground and in the classroom.
- What do you think he or she is like at home?

Jot down notes to show the character of that person. Don't use his or her name. Try to think of him or her from his or her point of view. Try to get inside his or her head. Do not write anything that would upset that person.

Appearance
The way he or she moves
What he or she says and how he or she says it
What he or she does and why
What he or she is thinking about

Use your notes to write a detailed character study of that person on the back of this sheet.

Learning intentions
To consider character.
To try to see things from another point of view.
To write a character study.

Outcomes

Difficulty level 2 3

Name Date

Describing settings

Read this extract about a kitchen in a block of flats carefully.

My Grandmother's Stories
by Adele Geras

First of all let me tell you about my grandmother's kitchen. It was a small square room with a large sink next to one wall and a wooden table pushed up to another. Because my grandmother lived on the third floor of a block of flats, the window in one wall was really a door and opened out on to a small balcony; and in jars tiny green cucumbers floated in a pale cloudy liquid, turning into pickles in the sunlight.

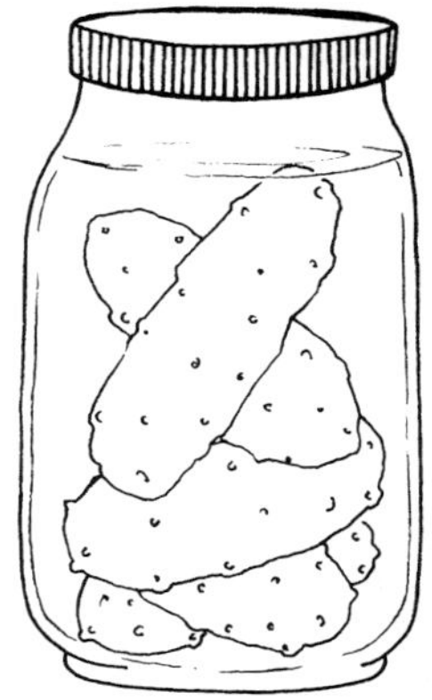

Write about a room that you know well, such as your bedroom, the kitchen or your classroom. Think about:

- the layout of the room
- what you see as you come into the room
- what is lit by natural and artificial lights
- why things are placed where they are
- the colours that you see.

Make the account your own personal viewpoint for a reader who has never seen the place you are describing.

Learning intentions
To use descriptive language.
To use personal experience to influence writing.
To describe a setting.
To consider the audience and try to keep its interest.

Outcomes

Difficulty level 1 2 3

Name Date

fold fold

My Diary	Monday	Tuesday ....
by		

Learning intentions
To write for a specific purpose and audience.
To develop character and to sequence events as diary entries.
To record imaginative emotional responses and write them in the first person.

Outcomes

Difficulty level
1 2 3

Write On 3

What are these riddles about?

Who am I?

I'm a curly-worly slitherer,
A wallower, a swallower,
A biter,
A spitter and a hitter
And a strike-with-all-my-mighter,
A squeezer sort of geezer,
Fond of strangulating seizure.
I'm a hisser not a kisser,
More alarming than I'm charming,
I'm something in the grass
That rhymes with … quake.

Sam McBratney

Who am I?

I am the oldest of the bears
but I will never die!
I wander slowly, silently
beneath the midnight sky.

I am the largest of the bears
I cannot sleep or fly
and yet I rest above the clouds
and dance when the moon is high.

I am the farthest of the bears
beyond the sun I lie
I wander with a million stars
I'm the Great Bear in the sky!

Judith Nicholls

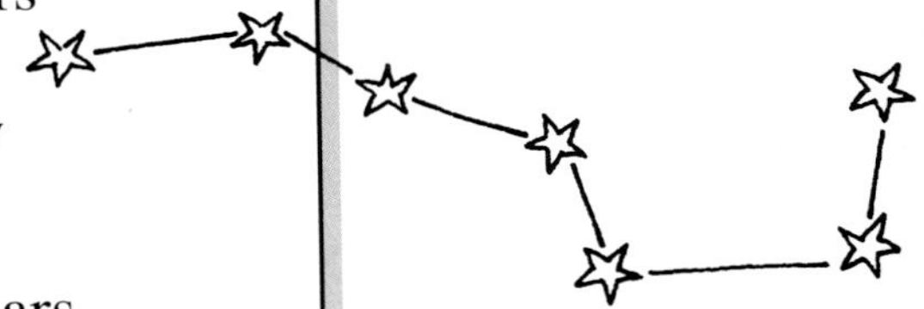

Write a riddle and shape it into a poem like these. Choose your words very carefully to build up a picture of your subject. You could try one of these subjects: cat, dog, car, rainbow or teacher.

Learning intentions
To use descriptive language.
To explore description that does not name the object.
To select vocabulary carefully.

Outcomes

Difficulty level 1 2 3

Write On 3

Haiku is a Japanese form of poetry. Its subject is often the natural world.

Did you see the moon,
stealthy as foxes, slip down
To the forest clouds?

Berlie Doherty

Daybreak

Faint glimmer of light,
Tries to overcome darkness,
Explodes into day.

Untouched blue blanket
Hovering above the world,
Waiting to fall down.

Fiery bursts of flame
Lighting up the universe
With burning glory.

Nikhala Kalra
(aged 10)

The haiku poem is very brief. It has seventeen syllables divided into three lines of five, seven and five syllables. Each line expresses a thought and every word is carefully chosen so that the whole poem creates a visual picture that captures a moment in time.

Write your own haiku. Try titles such as 'Snow', 'Night', 'Dawn' or emotions such as 'Anger' or 'Happiness'.

Learning intentions
To explore a specific form of poetry.
To consider syllables in the writing of a haiku.
To express visual imagery in words.
To consider poetry of other cultures and ages.

Outcomes

Difficulty level 1 2 3

Name Date

List poems

Some poems take the form of a list. The detail of the poems build up into a vivid picture.

In the poem 'He was...' John Cunliffe compiles an affectionate list of memories about his father.

He was...

He was...
a boy who became
a man,
a husband,
a father.

He was...
a good goalie,
a rotten batsman,
not bad at darts.

He was...
second cornet in the works band,
a man who brought his pay-packet straight home,
without stopping at the pub,
a man who enjoyed his dinner.

He was...
forgetful,
rarely on time,
sometimes tongue-tied,
at a loss at what to say.

He was...
always honest,
never sober at Christmas,
often puzzled by the world.

He was...
...my dad.

John Cunliffe

The poem 'Creation' reads like a recipe, listing the items as they are needed.

Creation

Make Universe.
Fill in stars
for decoration.
Put in planets.
Set sun alight.
Get cheese for moon.
Pour water and land
on earth.
Put ozone layer around.
Fill in gravity.
Put on humans and
animals.
All done.

Sam Turton (aged 10)

Compose a poem using a list-like form. It could be a list of things that irritate you or make you happy or unhappy. It could focus on night sounds, market-day or school assembly.

Learning intentions

To compile ideas and thoughts on a subject and make them into a list poem.
To broaden the range of styles of writing.
To use brevity of language for each item on list.

Outcomes

Difficulty level 1 2 3

Name Date

Snake

Snake
glides
through
grass,
over
pebbles,
forked
tongue
working,
never
speaking
but its
body
whispers,
listen.

Keith Bosley

Kite

I'm
part of a
project on flight.
I'm supposed to attain
a great height. But
unfortunately
I got stuck
in a tree
so
it
looks
like
I'm
here
for
the
night!

June Crebbin

These poems are arranged into the shape of the subject they are written about.
Write down some ideas on a topic or animal such as cat, tree, fish, sun, moon, butterfly or apple. Very lightly, draw an outline in the shape of your subject. Rework your ideas into the form of a poem and write them to fit the shape.

Learning intentions
To broaden the range of styles of writing.
To compile ideas and thoughts on a subject and make them into a poem.
To present that poem as the shape of its subject.

Outcomes

Difficulty level 1 2 3

Name Date

Read these poems.

Danger Sign

The notice said
WARNING!
THIS WATER IS POLLUTED
DO NOT FISH OR SWIM
THE OWNERS ARE NOT RESPONSIBLE FOR LOSS OF LIFE OR LIMB

So we gathered up our swimming gear
That we'd no longer need
And wondered should we tell them
That otters cannot read.

Pat Moon

Secretary Bird

Take a letter:

Say that
The ancient trees are falling,
Say that
the whale's song grows faint,
Say the passenger pigeon is gone,
The great auk is gone,
The rhino, the mountain gorilla,
Almost gone...

Dip your quill
In the sludge
Along the river,
In the soot
From the smokestack
In the poisoned lake,
In the burning rain.
Dip it in the blood of the great blue whale.

Take a letter bird:

To whom it may
Concern.

Alice Shertle

What thoughts and feelings do you have after reading these poems?

Choose an environmental concern of your own such as pollution or disappearing habitats. It could be something in the local environment or something worldwide. Shape your thoughts into a poem. Consider:

- what you want to say
- keeping the thoughts brief
- selecting your words carefully
- how you will end the poem
- how you want the reader to feel after reading it.

Concerns

Learning intentions
To consider poetry as a vehicle for raising issues and concerns.
To widen the range of style and structure of poetry.
To compile ideas and thoughts on a subject and make them into a poem.
To express visual imagery.
To consider the audience.

Outcomes

Difficulty level 1 2 3

Name Date

Read these two poems by Walter De La Mare.

Someone

Someone came knocking
    At my wee small door;
Someone came knocking,
    I'm sure — sure — sure;
I listened, I opened,
    I looked to left and right,
But nought there was a-stirring
    In the still dark night;
Only the busy beetle
    Tap-tapping in the wall,
Only from the forest
    The screech-owl's call,
Only the cricket whistling
    While the dewdrops fall,
So I know not who came knocking
    At all, at all, at all.

Walter de la Mare

The Listeners

'Is there anybody there?' said the Traveller
Knocking on the moonlit door;
And his horse in the silence champed the
    grasses
Of the forest's ferny floor:
And a bird flew up out of the turret,
Above the Traveller's head:
And he smote upon the door again a second
    time;
'Is there anybody there?' he said.
But no-one descended to the Traveller;
No head from the leaf-fringed sill
Leaned over and looked into his grey eyes,
Where he stood perplexed and still.
But only a host of phantom listeners
That dwelt in the lone house then
Stood listening in the quiet of the moonlight
To that voice from the world of men:
Stood thronging the faint moonbeams on the
    dark stair,
That goes down to the empty hall,
Hearkening in an air stirred and shaken
By the lonely Traveller's call.
And he felt in his heart their strangeness,
Their stillness answering his cry,
While his horse moved, cropping the dark turf,
'Neath the starred and leafy sky;
For he suddenly smote on the door, even
Louder, and lifted his head:
'Tell them I came, and no-one answered,
That I kept my word,' he said.
Never the least stir made the listeners,
Though every word he spake
Fell echoing through the shadowiness of the
    still house
From the one man left awake:
Ay, they heard his foot upon the stirrup,
And the sound of iron on stone,
And how the silence surged softly backward,
When the plunging hoofs were gone.

Walter de la Mare

These night-time poems both seem to tell an unfinished story set in an eerie and chilling atmosphere. Think about night-time and the eeriness of being alone at night. Express your feelings as a poem.

Learning intentions
To create an atmosphere in a poem.
To create a poem that tells a story.
To evoke an emotional response from the reader.

Outcomes

Difficulty level 1 2 3

Name Date

Applying for a job

Letters are written for all sorts of reasons. Some are personal letters to family and friends. Others are not personal and need to be written in a formal style.

Look at these job advertisements.

Many formal letters are written in response to advertisements for jobs. Which of these jobs would you like? Reread the advertisements carefully. Write a letter in response to one of these adverts.

Consider:
- layout and legibility of your letter
- politeness
- including details of your qualifications for the job
- how to convince an employer that you're the person they need.

Learning intentions
To write a formal letter.
To consider the 'tone' of a formal letter.
To consider content and style of letter.

Outcomes

Difficulty level 3

Name Date

Recipe

This is how Mum makes drop scones.

Mum takes a sieve and sieves 200g of flour into a bowl. She uses a 5ml spoon and adds one and a half spoonfuls of baking power and half a teaspoon of salt to the flour.

She then adds a 15ml spoonful of sugar to the ingredients. She makes a well in the centre of it all and adds a large egg and about 125ml of milk into the well.

She gradually works the dry ingredients into the wet until it all makes a smooth but very thick batter. Gradually she adds another 125ml of milk to thin the batter a little.

She greases a heavy frying-pan and heats it up. She drops spoonfuls of the batter into the frying-pan.

She cooks these for about 2 minutes until the top is covered with bubbles and then turns them over to cook on the other side.

About 2 minutes later they are ready. She spreads them with butter and jam. Just right for a tea-time treat.

Write a recipe for these drop scones. Your recipe should have a list of ingredients and the instructions for making them. Decorate the edges of your recipe when you have finished.

Learning intentions
To extract information from the storyboard.
To transfer this information into a specific type of information writing (a recipe).
To include listing of ingredients and the method of making.
To order the list of ingredients and sequence the instructions.

Outcomes

Difficulty level 1 2 3

Cities

Name Date

Look up these cities in an atlas.

Tokyo, Barcelona, Vancouver, Warsaw, Alexandria, Bombay, Berlin, Naples, Adelaide, Rio de Janeiro, Wellington, Santiago.

Answer these questions about each city.

Is it a capital city?
Is it by a river?
Is it on the coast?
Is it in Europe?
Is it an island?
Is it in the Southern Hemisphere?

Use the grid to record your answers.

Name of city	Capital city	By a river	On the coast	In Europe	In Southern Hemisphere

Answer these questions as full sentences.

1. How many cities are capitals?

2. How many of the capitals are also on the coast?

3. How many cities are situated by a river?

4. Are any cities not by a river and not on the coast?

5. How many capitals are by the coast?

Compose five more questions for a friend to answer.

Learning intentions
To write for another subject (geography).
To transfer information.
To answer questions in complete sentences.
To compose questions.

Outcomes

Difficulty level 1 2 3

Write On 3

Name Date

Read this weather forecast.

South
Cloudy but sunny periods developing. Occasional showers of rain or sleet possible. Maximum temperature 8°C.

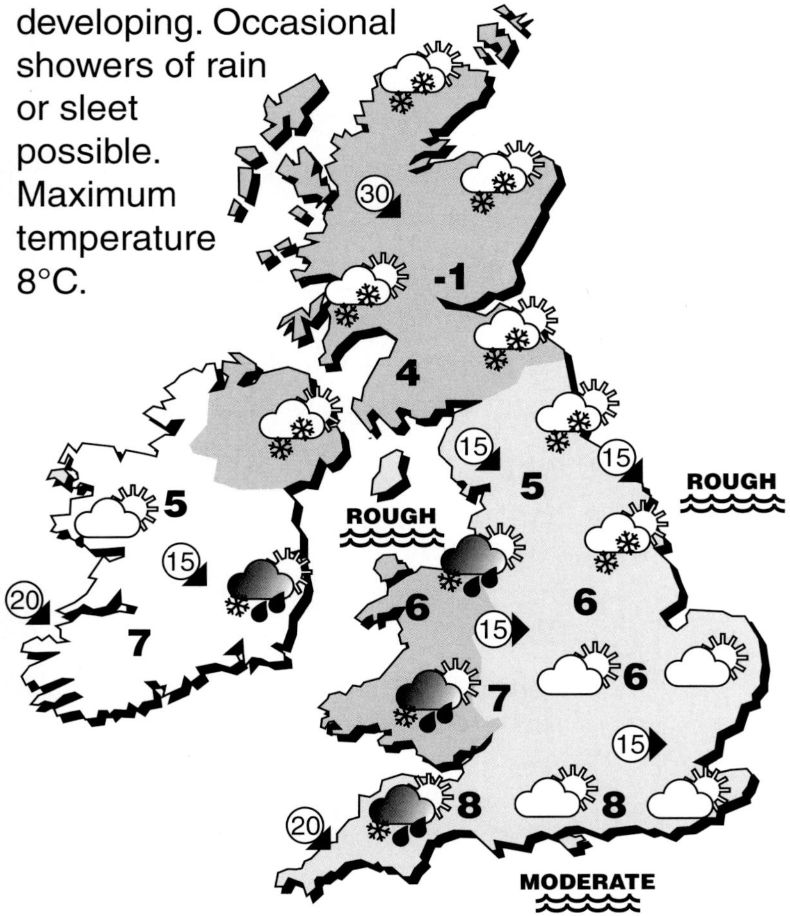

Use the weather map to write the forecast for other areas.

London and South East	North East and Yorkshire
South West and Channel Isles	North West
Midlands	Scotland
Wales	Ireland
East and East Anglia	

Learning intentions
To write for another subject (geography).
To transfer pictorial information into writing.
To use appropriate vocabulary.

Outcomes

Difficulty level 1 2 3

Write On 3

Name Date

Volcanoes

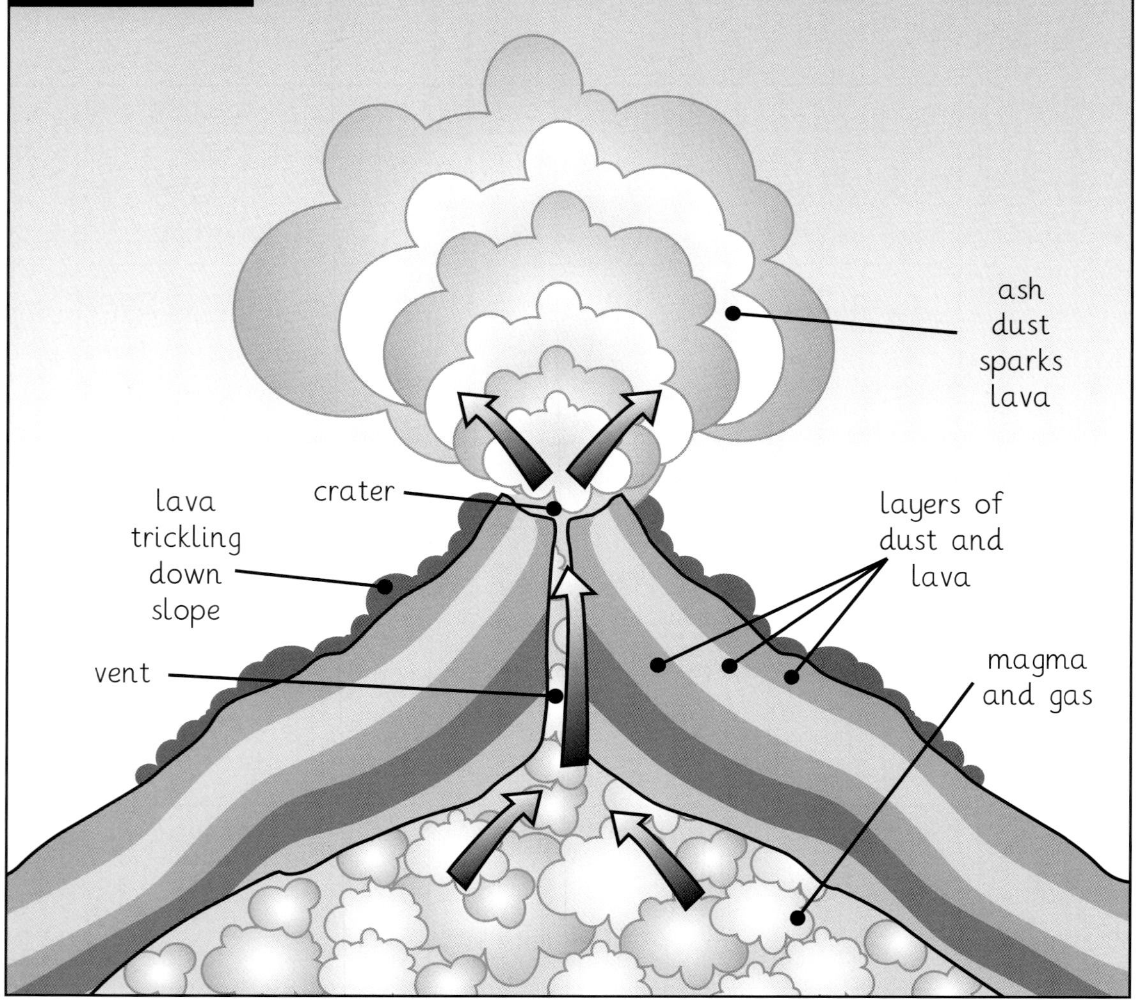

Study this diagram of a volcano carefully.
Extract information from the diagram and present it as a written account of an active volcano.
Use the glossary below to help you.

Consider:

- the use of headings and paragraphs to divide information
- how to describe the processes
- what detail to include
- the use of scientific terms.

Glossary

magma molten rock held deep inside the earth
vent a 'pipe' in the centre of the volcano
lava magma that has come to the surface through the vent
crater saucer-like hollow at the top of a volcano

Learning intentions
To write for another subject (geography).
To transfer pictorial information into writing.
To use appropriate vocabulary.

Outcomes

Difficulty level 3

Hot-air balloons

Name Date

Read this account.

French brothers Joseph and Etienne Montgolfier held their first public demonstration of an unmanned balloon flight at the marketplace in Annonay, France, on 4 June 1783. The Montgolfier family owned prosperous paper factories – this enabled them to finance their experiments. They had discovered that a large lightweight paper or fabric bag filled with heated air would rise.

A few months after their marketplace demonstration, on 19 September 1783, they repeated the experiment at Versailles. This time they used a larger balloon to carry the first airborne passengers: a sheep, a rooster and a duck.

Two months later on 21 November 1783, the first flight to carry people took place. Two men, Jean-Francois Pilatre de Rozier and Francois Laurent, flew up in a Montgolfier balloon and travelled over Paris. They burned a mixture of wool and straw under the opening of the bag to keep the balloon inflated with hot air. The flight lasted about 23 minutes and covered a distance of 9 kilometres.

After centuries of trying to develop some sort of flying machine, the first manned flight was made in a balloon. Imagine you are a television news reporter witnessing this first ever manned flight. Write a report of what you will say on television. Write it as if you are talking direct into the microphone.

Consider:

- how you will set the scene
- what the crowd and the atmosphere are like
- what you will say about the men that flew in the balloon and the flight
- what you will say about the Montgolfier brothers
- including brief interviews with, for example, people from the crowd, family and friends of the participants and the participants themselves.

Learning intentions

To write for another area of the curriculum (history).
To introduce other styles of writing.
To write from another perspective.
To use imagination to enhance factual information for the purpose of the writing.
To write in the present tense.

Outcomes

Difficulty level 2 3

Researching information

Name Date

Use this framework to help you sequence your information.

Topic ....

Through my own experience and class discussion I already know that ....

....

I was particularly interested in ....

....

I want to find out about ....

....

Through research using ....

....

I was able to find out ....

....

I now know that ....

....

Learning intentions

To consolidate known information.
To highlight gaps in knowledge and focus attention on them.
To consider special interests and select information accordingly.
To be aware of and build up a range of sources for finding information.

Outcomes

Difficulty level 1 2 3

Write On 3

Story pots

Name Date

Choose one or two ingredients from each pot and weave them into a story.

Plan the story carefully.

Consider:

- an interesting start
- character studies
- setting the scene
- introducing and explaining the dilemma
- resolving the dilemma
- changes in the characters
- a suitable ending.

Dilemmas **Characters** **Settings**

Learning intentions
To combine elements of character, setting and plot to create a story.
To consider the evolving nature of characters and plot.
To consider how character and setting influence the plot.
To write an imaginative story.

Outcomes

Difficulty level 1 2 3

Write On 3

Name

Date

Read this newspaper report.

Fire-fighters were called to a house on Acacia Avenue in the early hours of Wednesday morning to rescue a kitten stuck in a tree.

They were called to the scene by a member of the household who was awoken by the kitten's pitiful cry.

There were several unsuccessful attempts to rescue the kitten but eventually quick thinking by Johnny Birtwhistle, aged 8, saved the day, when he lured the kitten to the ground with a bowl of fish. 'I was so afraid for Poppet but thankfully she's safe and sound now!' said the kitten's owner, Joan Firkettle.

Now read this.

'Ladies and Gentlemen, I am so delighted to have been invited here today to this wonderful new wing of your community centre. The Christine Carruthers Centre has had a fine tradition of entertainment and social events and indeed you have surpassed yourselves with this fabulous exhibition today. Therefore it gives me enormous pleasure to dedicate this plaque to the life and work of our benefactor, declare this new wing open and welcome its new guests.'

What do you think is going on? Who do you think is giving the speech? Who would be at the occasion?

Imagine you are the news reporter. Write an account of this scene for your newspaper. Write it in columns like a newspaper and draw a 'photograph' to go with your story.

Learning intentions
To write in a specific style.
To write imaginatively.
To write in the past tense.

Outcomes

Difficulty level
1 2 3

Name Date

This story is written in sections. Read the first lines of each section of the story. What kind of story do you think it is? Think about the characters that might be involved. Where are they? What are they doing? Complete the story in the style and tense.

Fluff huddled into the warm grey coat of her mother, not daring to look at what it was that made the earth tremble beneath her paws. ....

'Fluff, Fluff where are you?!' his mother screeched, unable to conceal her panic. ....

It was several days since they had escaped from the orchard. Crossbones had taken charge and they gratefully followed him towards the mountains – but who knew of the perils that lay ahead? ....

So this was the place they had travelled so far to find. ....

Learning intentions
To consider and identify genre in story.
To continue story in appropriate style and tense.
To maintain suspense and create suitable links and endings for story.

Outcomes

Difficulty level 1 2 3

Name Date

Use this framework to help you create a science fiction story.

'Mission Control! Mission Control! Are you receiving me?' ....

As I had feared, the emergency fuel failed to ignite and my craft ....

I awoke in ....

'But I must return to my own people' ....

Sadly I turned my back on ....

Science fiction

Learning intentions
To follow a structure to write a science fiction story.
To consider the start of each paragraph and continue it.
To write in a specific genre.

Outcomes

Difficulty level 1 2 3

Planning sheet

Name Date

Use this framework to help you write your stories. Have you made a plan? Think about:

How will you start?

How will you end it?

If it is a story will it be a science fiction story? A fairy tale? An animal story? An adventure story?

Who is it for? Yourself? Your brother or sister? Someone in another class?

What sort of story will it be?

Where is it set?

Title ....

Who is going to be in it?

What is it going to be about?

What will happen?

You can use the plan to:
- write down all your ideas
- order your ideas
- remind you of what to write as you write
- structure your story.

You may find that ideas on your plan develop and change as you write.

Learning intentions
To plan a piece of writing.
To identify elements for a story.
To structure work.

Outcomes

Difficulty level 1 2 3

Write On 3

Name Date

Drafting your work

Drafting your work can help you to:
- clarify your ideas
- reflect on what you have written and change it if you need to
- change it to have a greater effect on the reader.

When you have written your first draft, read it and use the following questions to help you improve the content. Check it for spelling and punctuation.

1. Does your work make sense?
2. Are there words missing?
3. Does your story have a good start?
4. Can you add or change anything to make your story more interesting?
5. Can you use a more unusual and interesting word instead of the words you have used already?
6. What is the best part and why?
7. Is the ending right?
8. Have you remembered full stops, capital letters and speech marks?
9. Do all the sentences make sense?
10. Which words don't look as if they are spelt right? (Underline them.)

Now give your work to your response partner and listen to what he or she has to say about it. Read your work through one more time before presenting your final draft.

Learning intentions
To focus on and select elements of a story for improvement.
To appraise own work critically.
To alter work and revise ideas.
To proofread for spelling and punctuation.

Outcomes

Difficulty level 1 2 3

Name Date

This sheet has some suggestions for you to help your partner with his or her writing.

Drafting and redrafting writing

Ask your partner to read his or her writing aloud to you. While you are listening, think about:

- who it is written for
- the style and tone used to tell the story
- if it makes sense
- the effect the writing has on you: were you interested, excited, amused, entertained, sympathetic, moved, bored or losing interest?

Ask your partner some questions about their writing; maybe to clear up something you didn't understand or to ask for more information.

Discuss your response to your partner's writing. If she or he wants to make changes in response to your comments, give her or him time.

Editing

A partner will often spot mistakes which the writer has missed. Decide if you are going to write on your partner's manuscript or on a separate sheet of paper. Use these symbols and any of your own to help edit your partner's work.

Good word, phrase, paragraph or point ✓

Something which is not clear ?

Unwanted words ~~words~~

A word insertedΛ

Change of word or sentence order ⤻

Check the spelling <u>speling</u>

Editors' checklist

- Does it all make sense? Make any suggestions for changing content or layout.
- Which are the best parts and why?
- Does the writing need paragraphs?
- Is all the punctuation in the right place?

Full stops.

"Speech marks"

CAPITAL LETTERS

Question marks?

Commas,

Apostrophes it's

Learning intentions

To appraise the work of others critically, but in a positive way.
To provide support and encouragement to others.
To proofread the work of others.
To offer positive suggestions for improvement.

Outcomes

Difficulty level 1 2 3

Write On

I have finished all the activities in Write On 3.

Name______________________________ **Date**____________________

My favourite activity was ....

I liked it because ....

I found some activities difficult, such as ....

because ....

I have learnt how to ....

I would like to have more practice with ....